MW00967239

FINISHING LINE PRESS
www.finishinglinepress.com

IN EVERY CARNATION:
The Body of God

poems by

Barbara Knott

Finishing Line Press
Georgetown, Kentucky

IN EVERY CARNATION:
The Body of God

To Deena and Mary
with thanks for the
"Sex and Death and Beatles" poem
Barbara Knott

ISBN 978-1-63534-546-9 First Edition

ACKNOWLEDGMENTS

"Boxwood" was selected by Nikki Giovanni as winner of First Prize in the 2009 New *Millennium Writings*' Awards 28 poetry competition and published by *NMW*, with subsequent publication in the chapbook *Soul Mining*, Finishing Line Press, 2011.

The poems "Black Tulips," "Nightriding," "Water Chestnut," and "Morning Glory" previously appeared in the chapbook *Soul Mining*.

"Ladybugs" is the first poem in the University of Alaska's *Permafrost*, Issue 33, summer 2011.

"The Body of God" appeared in another chapbook, *MANTA Poems*, published by FLP in 2015, under the title "Two Ladies Discover Dali's Nuclear Mysticism."

"The Golden Orb Weaver" was published in Issue 10 of *Minerva Rising* (2016).

Variations of "Sex and Death and Beetles" as well as "Transcendental" were presented in *The Grapevine Art and Soul Salon* online literary/art journal, Issue 19, at www.grapevineartandsoulsalon.com.

Publisher: Leah Maines

Editor: Christen Kincaid

Cover Art: Sandy Mason

Author Photo: Jonathan Knott

Cover Design: Elizabeth Maines McCleavy

Printed in the USA on acid-free paper.
Order online: www.finishinglinepress.com
also available on amazon.com

Author inquiries and mail orders:
Finishing Line Press
P. O. Box 1626
Georgetown, Kentucky 40324
U. S. A.

Table of Contents

Preface....ix

I. FORTUNATE FALL

Forbidden Fruit....1
Falling Apple Morsel....2
Sex and Death and Beetles....4
Study in Roundness....9
Where Orpheus Sings....11
Apples in the Cellar of Dread and Desire....13
Boxwood....16
Water Chestnut....18
Cradle of Red Clay....20
A Pair of Gloves....22
Pregnant Woman Tending an Alchemical Oven....23
Black Tulips....24
Turtle....26
View from the Night....27
Returning to Our Senses....28
Winter....29
The God Secret....36
Lady Bugs....37
Alone, But Not Alone....38
Sonnet to Psyche....39

II. WELLSPRING OF LONGING

Under Closed Eyelids....43
Red Camellias....44
Hair Combing....46
Golden Orb Weaver....47
Snapdragons....50
Syntax of Love....52
Fox Eyes....55
Your Laughter....58
Nightriding....59

III. LOST AND FOUND

Changing Room....63
Transcendental....64
Woman with a Bowl of Grapes....67
Body of God....68
Morning Glory....79
The Feather....80
Luna Moths....81
Sweetgum Tree....82

Sources for Quotations in Preface....83

For my son Jonathan and the dream of the phoenix.

For the firefly whose light I took when I was a child and inclined to imitate what I learned from other humans without many questions except about how to do it: in this case, to place my finger against the luminous flesh that we called lightning, slide my nail under it and lift it away from the bug, and then to place the radiance on my ring finger like the jewel it was, only it had not the endurance of stone but lingered just long enough to see me home, watching the little light gradually fade into the darkness around me and then, still without thought, to wipe away its creaturely remains. Decades later, the firefly's rapidly diminishing kin, no longer blessing every child's last hour of the day outside in the dark with a yard full of tiny stars, would appear in congregation on film to remind me of the reverence I owe to every incarnation.

For the mystery of the invisible, unknowable, creative urge that stirs and shapes the multifarious forms and flesh of our existence on this darkly radiant, deeply sensuous, circling Earth, where we hope that curiosity, desire, compassion and creativity may help us to live in harmony with ourselves, with other humans, and with all that is incarnate in this more-than-human world. For the joy of co-creating in full-bodied love, wherever it can be found in nature and in the subtle body of imagination that we sometimes call soul.

PREFACE

Imagine a round table with a circle of chairs for guests, each bringing one memorable conversation piece:

Philosopher Joseph Dietzgen

There is ... something unknowable in every particle of nature, just as there is something invisible in every carnation.

Novelist and Poet D. H. Lawrence

God is the great urge that has not yet found a body
but urges toward incarnation with the great creative urge.
And becomes at last a clove carnation: lo! That is god.

Philosopher Rudolph Otto speaks of a **numinous experience as a nod from the gods.**

Poet W. B. Yeats describes his **vision of a rose in which each petal is a god.**

Poet Federico Garcia Lorca

Brown Christ/ passes from the lily of Judea/ to the carnation of Spain.

Mythologist and theologian David L. Miller

For images and imagination give body to things unknown and unknowable. ... Ideas, like relationships, often need body. From time to time they need coagulation, some face that we can face. And this is what the Trinity offers: the image of a God, who is love, which is ultimately triangular, giving body.

Is it not the case that when we are in love, images come?

Psychologist C. G. Jung

The real history of the world seems to be the progressive incarnation of the deity.

Poet T. S. Eliot

There is only the fight to recover what has been lost
And found and lost again and again.

Eliot's assertion turns Jung's thought about progressive incarnation into a spiral, the form that Jung himself embraced in writing. And so we spiral back to pick up what has been lost and found and lost again and again: the deep intuitional knowledge that whatever we call the gods or god or goddess or God is present in the world as we are present in the world and that our experience of the sacred comes through image and metaphor from nature.

Professor Susan Rowland, in her book *C. G. Jung in the Humanities: Taking the Soul's Path*, tells us, **Alchemists referred to this vision of human body and imagination indivisible from nature as the "subtle body": mind, body, and world co-creating, while the supposedly fixed boundaries between them are revealed as cultural, rather than actual.** Rowland draws on the work of Ann Baring and Jules Cashford in their comprehensive study *The Myth of the Goddess* to give us this view of the earliest known religious myth, that of the earth goddess: **She represents the sacred as immanent within nature and world. ... She stands for the divine as sexuality, embodiment, eros, connection, feeling, and love. ... Her incarnation can also be described as animism, the goddess as sacred nature in every tree, brook, or mountain. She speaks in many voices, woven together in a net or tapestry that forbids the privileging of any *one*.**

Imagination, which has the power to link visible with invisible and knowing with unknowing, gathers seed for plants and trees that flower and fruit, as well as clay for flesh, fur and feather. Images enable us to look through matter into mystery. Images and metaphors show us that God has body, subtle body, as subtle as the stardust from which we are made. Gods reveal their faces in all that lives and breathes and has being.

In all flowers, as in Yeats' rose, there is a root metaphor for discovering the body of God: *everygod*, for, as we hear from D. H. Lawrence, God is *cloven*, a cloven carnation, a flower named for its fleshy colors. Flowers nod to our meditative gazing, all the while beguiling us with what is unknown, invisible, in the landscape of our lives.

Flowers are also words. Poet John O'Donohue: **Words are like the god**

Janus, they face outward and inward at once. The flowering narcissus gets its name from a mythical figure who looks into nature and sees his own face looking back at him. The human gaze is full of longing. Our longings find lavish expression in Greek Eros, the god of love, whose energy is sensuous, carnal, and directed toward the mystery of otherness.

Philosopher and ecologist David Abram: **If we do not soon remember ourselves to our sensuous surroundings, if we do not reclaim our solidarity with the other sensibilities that inhabit and constitute those surroundings, then the cost of our human commonality may be our common extinction.**

Someone arrived unexpectedly at the table to contribute her quotation, one that I found in Gaston Bachelard's *The Poetics of Reverie* (Boston: Beacon Press, 1960, p. 155). Poet Anne-Marie de Backer, *Les etoiles de novembre:*

He left me all I need to live
His black carnations and his honey in my blood.

This collection of poems is my floral arrangement for the table of talk about what matters. Some poems emerge, like flowers, in tight, compressed forms that unfold as they are warmed by the reader's gaze. Others show their colors on vines that creep and twine, trail and dangle, like long and shaggy thoughts. Some are made for gazing while they unfold in place. Others have some shag and beg to be followed until the mind's spiraling journey returns to a pausing place. Please join me in this conversational adventure. Imagine yourself as one among these honored guests.

Welcome All!

I.
FORTUNATE FALL

FORBIDDEN FRUIT

Some say it was an apple
the fruit God forbade Adam and Eve.
Can't you imagine the first woman sheltering
(from all that sweltering light)
in the shaded garden, that Eden
in name so like Eve that she must have taken
the scent of fruit and musk to be her own
even though she'd been warned
to forego learning, to remain dormant
in the rib of Adam?

Some say it was a pomegranate.
That makes sense to me, for the apple
we know now is too tame
to hold the allure of Edenic darkness
that came disguised as a serpent
with a tongue for talking and for licking
a tail for writhing like a pole dancer
around the knowing tree, an arrowed head
for piercing the virgin mind of Eve.
Can't you see her exploring the fruit

turning it in her newfound hands
knowing it by touch of flesh on flesh
by the blood red color she sees
even in her blushing fingertips? How she
is startled when, of their own accord
fingers split pomegranate and spill seeds
plump waterladen arils
and then bring them to her mouth to feed
her hunger, their exotic juice quenching
thirst she didn't even know she had?

FALLING APPLE MORSEL

When told that all the world
believed him wise
Socrates said he was wise
only in that he knew how much
he did not know.
I realize how much we take for granted
sometimes when I try to explain
some things to my Pekingese pups.

For example
I was standing on the floor furnace
allowing heat to travel up under
my robe when I noticed both of them
the black grumpy one and the tawny optimist
staring up at me as if I'd forgotten
I was supposed to be following
them to the kitchen

which in fact I had
being made suddenly shivery
as I crossed the furnace grate
where I stopped and stood in thought
hands behind me just so
until the dogs came back and found me
in a place where they could not go
and I started to tell them things

they need to know like
You can't stand on the grate
because you don't have shoes
Only humans have shoes.
And even then I could hear the talky one
saying back to me
Only those who don't grow
their own fur need heaters.

Our interspecies conversation
takes us to breakfast where
when they have finished bowls
of lamb and rice and crisp crackers
I have to explain
as they watch me eat
my apples and peanut butter
that dogs don't like apples.

To prove that
I hold a morsel of apple
to the nose of the extravert
standing on hind legs
and leaning against my knee.
He agrees
wondering though
How about the peanut butter?

And the apple morsel falls
from my fingers to the floor
where the introvert
tongues and swallows it
thus proving once again
that unlike Socrates
I still don't know
how much I do not know.

SEX AND DEATH AND BEETLES

Curbside, near the hair salon
I find a beetle
two inches long and a half inch wide
legs in the air and rigid.
I know in a moment it is dead
and soon find out how light it is to hold
how compelling in color:
a glossy tan runs along the back of its head
and large folded wings, covered with random
black spots like a rich, enameled pin
dropped by someone in a hurry.
The discovery thrills me.

I take the beetle inside
where the new girl at the desk squeals
and backs against the wall.
She is not ready to hear
that this thing I have in my hand
is harmless to humans
or that it is dead. In her mind
it might at any moment creep. Oh, God!

Deena, not so fearful, still
performs a jittery dance
on her way to see what I have
while the scared one asks, "What is it?"
in a high voice from the corner, and I say
"I think it's a rhinocerous beetle."

Now more attracted than repelled
she slides like a limbo dancer
under an invisible bar of fear
back to the computer, chanting
"I'm going to look it up! I'm looking it up!"
and finds it is what I think and more:
it has some kin named Hercules
that grows five inches long.

Deena's mother Mary phones
from the shampoo bowl in the back room
to ask the cause of the commotion.

I say I want to take the beetle home
and give it a royal tomb befitting
its ancient lineage in Egypt.
Deena brings me a ziplock bag.

We are settling down
when she with a strand of my hair in her hand
starts to tell me about dating a Cuban once
and interrupts herself to ask
"Have you ever had a Cuban boyfriend?"

which, to her surprise, I have:
eighteen, newly met at college
Raul invited me home
to an apartment in Atlanta
full of uncles and cousins planning
their return to Cuba where they would
join Castro's revolutionary army.
That day they were too busy
in their fantasy of war
to notice ardent hands
maneuvering along the sofa's back.

To Deena I simply say "Yes!"
only briefly stopping her excited tale
about a Cuban "stallion" that veers off
into the story of what she saw one day
on opening the unlocked door of the salon
restroom where her overwrought male client
was relieving himself of pentup sexual pressure
and Deena screamed and the madman
dogged her for years, saying in public
every time he caught up to her

"I want to see you naked."

Deena was wearing a short skirt
and stiletto heels just like she has on now
at the time she styled the man's hair
so I don't know what else she expected

but anyway her story reminds me
of one told by another friend
who went to Cuba and slept
with her motel bedroom window open
where a man leaned in during the night
and said "I want to sex you!"

What do beetles have to do with sex?
I started by bringing up the beauty
of the dead beetle, so like a costly ornament
made to adorn a woman's breast, secure her allure.
But a live beetle is set for sex of its own kind:
the small creature with uniquely patterned wings
sups on nectar and fruit
and clears the feeding ground to mate.

Two horns
one from the thorax and one from the head
meet to make a prodigious weapon
with which it throws a competing male
off a tree limb and goes along
to climb and sex the female
sometimes, we read
taking up to an hour to do it.
Imagine that!

And also, in the article I am reading
the rhinocerous beetle is identified as the
strongest animal on earth
meaning it can carry 850 times its own weight.

Think of an elephant carrying that many elephants
on its back or a person lifting 180,000 pounds
(the same weight as six full double-decker buses
the article says).

We can see that strength being tested on
the Internet: a video clip of a rhino beetle
outfitted with a leaden backpack
walking on a tiny treadmill.
I swear it's true!
Some scientists figured out that when
the beetle is burrowed with his mate
it would take l,141 other beetles to pull him
out of her love tunnel.

Science doesn't teach us much about passion
but the subject interests me, in insects and
otherwise, and so I learn by reading until
the hands-on experience comes again

toward evening when
I climb my back steps in the falling dark
and see on the porch
a shadowy form—no two, conjoined—
a pair of beetles so still I think they are dead
until I touch one and hear a hissing squeak
of protest (they have another half hour to go
I guess) and move through the door
thinking how the world is marvelous.

I ask once more
why does a dead beetle
engender in the hair salon
such earthy conversation
and in my mind such pondering
on the ways of the world?

My own answer is this:
the beautiful and strong among us
however small
remind us that we are alive
and that in death
lacking an exoskeleton like that
of the beetle now in the ornate box
beneath my table lamp
we humans leave behind at best
some trace of character
we have fashioned
from passionate living and loving
conjoined with mirthful moments
attached to which, we hope
are hints of grace and at least
a trace of elegance.

STUDY IN ROUNDNESS

On the pebbled patio outside my window
a squirrel worries the birdfeeder
suspended from a shepherd's crook
carving a footwide curve of space over
a small transparent disk supported by dark
metal rim and bars that keep it centered.

The acrobatic animal displays
its roundness in sundry ways:
by perching atop the crook, back
arched, tail raised in a fountain of fur
small round head notched with ears alert
to sudden sounds, and then all quiet

diving to hang upside down
and hold the disk like a planet
rolling between left hind foot
across anus, up right leg and foot
to where claws meet to make a circle
below which the plumb-dropped rascal

of a rodent swings his roundbellied body
toward the dangling blue glass sphere
and grabs the nearest seed to feed
his lucky little gullet this Sunday morning
while the scarlet-plumed cardinal scolds
him roundly from a nearby limb.

Birds are full of roundness, too:
curvaceous bodies support varieties
of beaks and sartorial arrangements
of plumes and fans and downy soft underwear.
If you follow them home, there
you will find roundness nestified.

I have heard that birds shape the inside
of nests by pressing their breasts against

the mashy tree debris they bring with their
beaks, building places with soft corners
to contain eggs until they hatch
and to house fledglings before they fly.

My round reverie is rattled now
by the rocking of the shepherd's crook
and a sideways flight of gray squirrel
a fluttering of red wings
a fall of birdfeeder ball and spilled seeds
a sudden swooping down of birds

large and small, none so bright as the cardinal
who gets what he wants and darts away.
And if soul is round, as Van Gogh's
swirls in his Starry Night suggest,
the squirrel in his feeder-robbing rounds
satisfies not only belly but soul.

WHERE ORPHEUS SINGS

On the side of a mountain
my father stands with finger
and thumb lightly resting on the brim
of an old fedora
that curves against his palm
his mind serene from all I can tell
there in the land of shades.
In my dream, I am higher up
inside a room with a too-bright light
watching him through a glass pane.

Drawing close in the twilight
come denizens of wilderness
and woods: squirrel, deer
butterfly, beetle, spider
turtle, snake, owl
pigeon, crow
a crocodile, some fireflies:
familiars who attend to my father
and he to them in a reverie that is
soundless, at least to my human ear.

I long for the cool moist glass
to hold me, but curiosity hushes fear:
What is taking place out there
in the dark where Nature's creatures
gather, circled and silent, gazing, rapt?
A mutual listening reveals a murmuring
under the silence, song-like or seeking
sound, searching for words, and in my own
quiet sigh, I find myself thinking:
Turn out the light.

Open the door into the night. Trust
the moon and stars to show what
can be seen and, below all, listen
at this place between two worlds
where Orpheus sings the cry of the panther
the trill of the whippoorwill
and the song of two-footers who hold
in their imagination and in their hands
what will make, for good or ill, worlds
upon worlds upon worlds.

APPLES IN THE CELLAR OF DREAD AND DESIRE

May 21, 2011

Lately, we have been overborne
with news of Nature's cataclysmic
ways: aftermath of a mine collapse
in Chile, earthquakes in Haiti
and the Orient, a tsunami's
waves washing over Japan's leaking
nuclear plants, radioactive fish
imagined to be flashing toward our shores.

Now one disaster close to home:
tornados roll through Alabama
into Georgia, destroying Ringgold
a town my father loved, disturbing
grounds of Berry College in Rome
twenty miles from where my mother's
tornado dread told her a thousand
times that any minute she'd be dead.

In a storm's approach she could see
black crows clawing air and cawing doom
come to take her breath away. She swore
no sucking wind should slay her like
a cat stealing an infant's breath
one way her Irish kin believed
the stern-faced Father in Heaven
might reclaim what He had given.

Beatrice was her name. She didn't
know her namesake Beatricé
object of Dante's immortal
desire, and was not in her own eyes
the great love of anybody's life.
My mother learned early that she
likely would not perish from some
common violence caused by man:

neither a hearth fire that consumed
baby William her brother nor
when she was five, by tongues of flame
from a wood stove that licked off her dress
and burned her tender thighs, forever
mingling dread and desire, nor even
when she was grown and married
and told the Law where to look for whiskey

traps that hid her husband's father's
hooch, the gunshot that struck the well
windlass where she stood drawing water—
warning her to hold her tongue. No, it
was Nature she feared anytime
a clear day turned cloudy, reminding
her that creatures could be thunder-struck

or speared by lightning's crack and flare

or worst of all, blown by outrageous winds
out of nesting places and undone.
Not long after I was born, wanton
winds rushed in from the peach orchard
toward our small house. She wrapped me
from head to toe and pushed through corn
stalks that clutched her clothes, stumbling
all the way to the Big House

where my uncle shook from me a sharp
intake of breath, a second birth.
Despite these frequent shocks that proved
the chaos of her world, she lived
eight decades exposed and vigilant
while she watched for wind to rise
and paced from door to door, retreated to
her childhood fear, entered the cellar there

and knelt in darkness smelling of apples
dried for sauce and cakes, keened
Ah me! Oh my! until the wind died
and she was free again to breathe, again
to love her life. I am glad
these late titanic twisters blew in
long after her peaceful death
or shapeshifting dread surely would

have bullied her fugitive heart
to a less dignified stopping.
Now, while I write these words, floods
cover Mississippi. Cynics
watch news of apocalypse collapse
into a joke on an old man who
predicted the world would begin
its end today in global quakes.

Like the cynic, he does not know
that soul is where worlds rise, fall
and rise again to build a bridge
between dread and desire.
Watching my mother's fretful way
of rehearsing death released me
from her drama of dread and let
my own desire find living room.

Now, when winds uproar and dark
clouds gather, when thunder cracks
and rain soaks soil, I inhale
a deep draught of apple-scented air
from the cellar of my mind, open
the door, breathe the world and let it
breathe me, knowing that I will die
someday, but never dreading that, never.

BOXWOOD

My grandmother
Della by name
died. Her remains
besides her graveyard bones
include one of two boxwoods she planted
sixty years ago in front of a porch
big enough to hold a rocking chair
where I, a child sitting on the plank steps
learned her rock-and-spit cadence that
sometimes, in the forward motion,
sent a stream of tobacco juice
past my ear to the ground.

Neglected for forty-five years
the hard-stemmed evergreen bush stood
stubborn while house collapsed
outbuildings decayed
gardens returned to riot
unpruned shoots became old growth.

The solitary shrub takes me back
to her sanctuary of pendulum clock
and featherbed, of quilting frame
and wood stove, teacakes, apple cakes
and a small brown crockery vase
that sits now near the clock
in my own safe place.

On the porch when I was young
she let me try her snuff and laughed
like a local Baba Yaga
though not unkindly
when I threw up on the ground beside
that same boxwood bush.

In her back yard, next to the outhouse
round black washpots stood beside
a woodpile. When rains came
zinnia beds thrived
on compost tea that seeped
to all the roots, including mine.
I was long preoccupied with her burial.

In dreams
I dislodged her body
from roadside layers of stone
and on my shoulders carried her home
to decaying house
watery gardens
boxwoods that marked
her place on earth

and my first hints
that a carefully pruned life lacks
what the ragged boxwood shows

(when I could tell her truth
she let me go):

some things need to grow
sometimes unchecked.
Grim attention to the tidy turning out
of wildering bush or child
prevents those long and shaggy thoughts
that shape the soul.

WATER CHESTNUT

(Trapaceae)

On the river shoreline
a tree retains

the splendor of spring leafing
seems simply startled by winds

that plucked it from the ground
roots upturned now

undignified, exposed, and likely to die
in unbecoming posture.

In my heart, a lump of bitterness
torn from a tempestuous

turning away of love.
In my hand, a black nut

foraged from debris thrown up by the river
during the past month's storms.

The chestnut fits my palm.
It does not look like a seed

or rattle like a seed pod.
Not round and brown and friendly

like the ones we roast and eat, it seems instead
a castoff of some force contracting the universe

downward, inward toward cessation.
Only with caution can one caress

the nigrescent form.
Four right-angled horns discourage intimacy.

The points are like a cat's claws extended but
the nut won't make a pad for me

like a cat will, if coaxed.
Still, it moves.

One view evokes a torso
Victorian, stiff

in lowcut armored gown inset with pleats.
The missing head suggests a child's anger

the mutilation of a doll.
Turning it another way I see

a crowned and bearded porcine face
snout flanked by pointed earlike indentations.

The corners of my mouth
lift and then

a lightening of the rest of me:
a shadow's weight

of infinite withholding
lay darkly in my hand

until the shape began to play
retrieved my heart

from a grave, unholy place and filled it
with a new and stormed-out morning.

CRADLE OF RED CLAY

We watch them lower your father
into the ground, newly dug:
a flat-sided tomb of red clay
not loose and composted for a thing
to grow but tamped hard to house
a steel coffin and the slow moldering
of flesh and bones. We want to ask
what is time to a departed soul?

All around us is hard, shovels
and lumps of clay, not malleable
like the stuff we are said to be shaped
from, but resistant to receiving
this body back. Our hearts labor
at letting go. Comfort comes
from the lazy drift on a nearby lake
of three swans and half a dozen ducks.

Patient attendants steer the body
down and down, then loosen bulky gray
rigging and tenderly draw that up again.
Shifting, lifting, they remove all
supports around the grave, fold the grass
rugs, and there your father, six feet
below us, himself a chemist
prepares to undergo his final

experiment in dissolution.
His coffin, a metallic gray color
resembles in some way Nature's chrysalis:
selfmade container for transforming
earthen worm to soulbearing insect
that flies. With that thought, the grave
they put him in no longer seems so alien.
A yellow butterfly appears, to remind us

how Greek Psyche got her name and we
our name for soul. We speak of your
father's soul lingering to see
if he can say with us *well done.*
Voices drain away as mourners leave.
Words sympathetically spoken
now change focus to lighter, more
everyday concerns like work and food.

The few phrases that float back to
our ears are about real estate
and lunch at the Picadilly.
We take from the blanket of roses
two and toss them onto the coffin
then bend to collect a few loose clods
crumble them in our hands and scatter
dirt across the middle of a vast red cradle

that holds now the remains of a man
who chose the Prayer of St. Francis
for his funeral, thereby himself
honoring his eight decades
as a gentle creature. Only when
the butterfly drifts away do we
feel it is over, this farewell gesture
toward all we have known of him.

We follow murmuring mourners
to make selections of meat loaf
corn bread, country fried steak and rolls
sweet and unsweet iced tea, to weigh
values of investment and return
and to wait our turns in the long queue
that leads back to funeral parlor
tent and grave, and to that vapor trail
that trace of soul left by the butterfly.

A PAIR OF GLOVES

Death turns us inside out.
And yet I know no death
can take me from you
or you from me, finally and forever.

Let death be like the peeling of a glove
and let us be a pair. The first glove off
waits while the other uses up its wear.

Intuition says the journey
will let us meet again somewhere
for I am shaped by you and you by me
to find again each in the other.

PREGNANT WOMAN TENDING AN ALCHEMICAL OVEN

Title of Drawing, Anonymous, probably Medieval

She muses, and somewhere in her belly stirs
a meeting, a sigh.
Oh my lover, my soul brother,
spirit driven, sense sodden
our destinies have found us.
We are no longer two, but three.
She is content.

I am here in this house
that belongs to you, my lover
tending an oven
where salmon bakes slowly
distilling juices that will linger
on fingers fetching morsels from plate to lips.
Old spirit chemists
spoke of turning lead to gold:
I wait upon the bright gold
of the man you want to be
and the burnished gold
of the woman I will become:
man, woman
waiting for grace
three graces
to dance
to move forever
between sacred and profane
among the salt waters
of our coming and our weeping.

We have made this room, you and I
This oven, you and I
We have our loaves and fishes
and our cat, you and I.
I am content.

BLACK TULIPS

In my early spring garden
full of tall-stemmed buds
black tulips at first resemble others
compact and green, concealing colors.

A brilliant display of orange
erupts among their large-cupped cousins
clad, on closer look
in swirls of yellow and pink
breathtaking debut beside the birdbath.

Two round gray pots hold
a dozen whites in one, and in the other
a cluster called Queen of the Night
rare and without hint
of what moved Nature to try
in flowers this uncommon hue.

The early ones arrive without fuss
welcome and white and lovely.
I wait on the latecomers until
dark depths ooze
through green petals and stain them black.

In Manet's painting of a gypsy
playing guitar, lively blacks compel
a long look, and so do these
flowers of darkness named for a queen
in Mozart's *The Magic Flute*
whose voice enters the ear
like black tulips strike the eye:
dramatic, ravishing, rendering
all else mute.

I think of Rilke's love of darkness
from which we come
into the world and then return
taking with us
not nothing
but all the colors we have
yearned for, blushed and bled
and burned for in our time.

TURTLE

A dormant firepit now banked with ferns
holds ashes of a turtle
that I, driving, saw at last
then swerved to let it live
and felt the jolt of its undoing.

Ancient ones say a turtle's shell
supports the world, but they did not
foresee machines like this car
weighted down with bagged garden soil
catching the slow ones crossing—

creatures so complex in the making
shaped out of bone and flesh
blood and breath.
How quickly this one comes undone
and pays the price of my distraction.

Turtle parts scattered: mushroomed
phallic head, eyes locked in shock. Cracked
shell upended like a fractured fruit bowl
reveals organs soft like mine and rosy.
Scraped raw now, they cannot be restored

but spill instead across bloody boundaries, back
into the All from which they may come again
as stone or star, robin or rosebud, phallus or fern
or a bright bowl of oranges on a table underneath
a painting of a girl in saffron-colored gossamer gown

asleep on a bank by the sea
dreaming, gestating, ripening
inside some fertile force that may turn
things-to-do into things-to-be and be with:
a deeper noticing.

VIEW FROM THE NIGHT

Awake
an unsettled evening's
remembered moan recedes:

eyes attuned to inscape
I see again the night's
dream images.

Above, stars scatter.
Below, they brighten
eyes of fish in a river shoal.

On shore
a goat browses bark
from a tall pine tree.

Far off, the imagined silver scent of starfire.
Nearby, the brown stench of river rot.
Very close, musk from the dappled buck

who interrupts his ruminating
to strike the ground
Panlike with his hoof

flushing a starling
from its treetop roost
while a watersnake slides into the deep.

Snake, bird, goat, fish and star:
when I come to my senses
I am no longer stuck in the problem of me.

RETURNING TO OUR SENSES

The eye declares

what is beautiful and approachable.

The ear notices

noise, song and silence.

Nose and tongue offer

fragrance, taste.

Touch teaches us

what to do with appetite.

WINTER

Scenes in slow motion mark the mood
of a brooding mind.
Winter is, above all, a season of interiority.

(1)

Listening to shards
of ice bristling
like needles clicking
in a cosmic knitting of weather and world
she moves away from the window
of her living room in Nyack, New York
and its view of snow falling against a backdrop
of pale sky: a vanishing world, white on white
to a glass door
that lengthens the scene, shows the storm's
soft siftings on the dark Hudson River.

Snow conceals and reveals.
A solitary bark hurled her way
is her only clue that there is a dog
on the path beside the river.

(2)

On the path beside the river
walking to work takes her through village
and past a snow-covered theater
now closed for renovations.
From the peak of the pediment
comes an uncanny sound, a coo
that bursts and hangs in heavy air.
A fatbreasted pigeon flies into view.

Two days ago she saw a hawk wheeling
above a house near Hook Mountain.
All birds become spectacular in winter

when bare trees fork the sky and winter's blood
becomes a river not surging
but slow like the flow of stone.

(3)

Slow like the flow of stone
she makes her way to the downstairs door
of a church housing a school for children
ages two to six
and prepares to greet them

coming in through the garden
where their mittened fingers reach out
to a rosemary bush planted near the door
pinching here and there a leaf.
Entering the room, they stamp their feet
to knock cold slush from shoes
remove mittens and wraps, setting loose
the sharp scent of evergreen.

(4)

The sharp scent of evergreen lingers
for long moments while they stand
with eyes dilating to take in tables
richly set for learning.

Still dreaming hands
locate shining bell
blue rectangle, paint brush
piano keys, a map of Spain,
things that draw them each
to a child's work:
interplay of hands and mind.

Adults complain
that there is so much to do and so little time.

For children
time is always a long moment and momentous.

(5)

Time is always a long moment and momentous
high up in the studio above the classroom, where
in another interplay of mind and hands
two women make space for art
and gods to come in.

Their collaboration is a dance
with first one leading, then the other:
two circles of overlapping energy
that form the almond-shaped mandorla,
a wellspring of imagination
out of which come masks and figures
dramas and ceremonies.

At ease in each other's company, they are
mutually intent today on separate occupations:
artist finishing a mask of Greek Demeter
writer planning how words will fill the mask.
The maskmaker stands in natural light
coming through the window
on this gray day. The scribe works away from
the window, by lamplight.
Dark dances lightly between them.

(6)

Dark dances lightly between them:
One sets Demeter's mask aside
and turns her dreaming hands toward earth.
The room's silence is punctuated
by the startling sound of clay
being thrown onto a table—
an ancient rite required to claim

earth's collaboration with the maker.

The other lifts the mask to her own face
and begins to dream: the mythic mother's story
says her daughter, abducted by Hades
Lord of the Underworld
and made his queen
is absent from the earth this time of year
and so the goddess of fruit, flower, and grain
full of dread and bitterness
deprives us for a time of all that grows.

What then? Standstill? Retrograde?
When growth is not the game, where do we go?
Inward? Where seeds lie deep
and dormant, hard with potential, and hold
the gift of dreaming?

(7)

The gift of dreaming:
two women dreaming.
One watches a windowpane
prevent snowflakes
from tangling in the lace.

Suddenly, a low insistent rumble
slow in saying who or what it is, thunders
a threshold between parallel worlds
of myth and weather.

The friends respond as one
to sudden whistling of wind.
Their round eyes now
are locked in wondering
whether nature has cracked its hide
and if so, who are they?

(8)

Who are they?

The soul's wintry turning yields
a pigeon's coo and thunder
a bark, a clap, bursting seams
a struggling, gurgling thrust
of consciousness.

Sound draws the lover of words
to a window behind the sculptor's table
where she refuses to glance directly down
at what the other does:
no signal yet that time is past
when gaze or word would be intrusion.

Now, the shaper says and nods
toward where her hands are spread.
The goat-god makes his way
out of a gray mass of clay, haunches first, manly
and as uncompromising as his handler is
in her desire to give him living room.

Reverie returns the other's thoughts to Greece.

(9)

Reverie returns her thoughts to Greece
and to Psyche, whose story
complicates love and loss
until, despondent, the girl tries
to drown herself. The stream refuses
and delivers her instead to rustic Pan
earth god, advocate for life
in this world who, when we despair
that we have not the will or force to live

returns us to our senses

as he did Psyche
by urging her into hard soul-making work.
She must appease jealous Aphrodite
who assigns formidable tasks
impossible to achieve without creaturely help:

to sort a barn full of mixed grains
to gather golden fleece from testy god-owned rams
likely at any moment to lash out
and lacerate her mortal flesh
to fill a cup with water from a mountain cleft
requiring wings to reach
and then descend into the Underworld—oh, woe!
and bring a box of beauty back from the depths
for beauty's queen, Aphrodite

before Psyche can claim
the jealous one's son, the Lord of Love
now out of reach and languishing.

Will she?

(10)

She will
with help from ants
and reeds, tower and eagle
and dauntless courage of her own.

Psyche returns from the Underworld
holding the box of beauty.
Instead of yielding it yet to Golden Aphrodite
she applies a touch first to her own face
and falls into oblivion
where Eros finds and restores her to himself

and to the gods: a metamorphosis and a paradigm.

And who from Hades comes
with pomegranate seeds between her teeth?
Persephone, pulled by her mother's desire
makes her way home.
Her season's journey to console the mother
thaws the frigid earth and brings
a gathering of tender green anticipation.

(11)

A gathering of tender green anticipation:
Downstairs, the children play and work
work and play.
A child listening to a seashell
hears murmuring from the soul.

So soon we forget the compelling need
of those inchoate eyes to construct a world
from inward laws, forget the soul's desire
for sacred space where time is leisure to build
and take apart and build again.

Winter wakens us to what
the children show:
to be alive and fully human
is to deepen life with slow motion
by looking on the inward sphere
and in momentous time to muse on
imagination's wealth, Hades' gold.

(12)

Winter is, beneath all, a season of interiority.

THE GOD SECRET

Where to look, then
for the God secret?

Is it outside or in?
Either or both?

The climate says, Look here!
and Over There!
and even Yonder!

Wonder may be
the theme to ponder
in winter.

LADYBUGS

Jostled
by human hand
ladybugs
red lacquered
oval shells
black spots
fall
one leaf
to another
inseparable
they mate.

ALONE, BUT NOT ALONE

We are compelled
by longing
we creatures whose coupling
gives birth to our world.

This morning
in the woodwork of my lofty room
persistent rhythmic pigeon cries
penetrate light, uneasy sleep.

I lie for a long while
listening to sounds
suffused with images
of bird, feather, and hot blood

of pecking and tugging
climbing and flexing
an edifice of strife:
a final rub and then

in a tiny terrible spurt
a small death
the seed is passed that gives
a pearly luster back to life.

SONNET TO PSYCHE

One mask of God is called by ancient Greeks
Eros, Lord of Love, whose arrow springs
from yearning, brings a trembling shock that seeks
to rock a universe until it sings
stories we call myths, paradigms
for all we know that's personal and rare.
Closest to our hearts, the tale that charms
a secret from the hidden god: fair
Psyche, like her curious sister Eve
goes where gods forbid and whirls about
and suffers torment while she learns to grieve.
Aphrodite turns her inside out.
Psyche's gaze, a window on the world:
the grit that scrapes the mollusk grows the pearl.

II.
WELLSPRING OF LONGING

UNDER CLOSED EYELIDS

Under closed eyelids lies
a dreamscape framed by sea and sky
lifeless until a broad tree shudders
from root to fruit and seed.

Rough bark breaks to make thick gray
slabs like books where figures come forth
dim at first then clearly
dimensional: they move in slow

motion toward the shoreline where
a naked woman emerges from the sea
footprints springing flowers
fingertips releasing doves.

Those who would be lovers
follow her and make
songs of petition
and praise.

Oh Lady of the Sea
fill us with desire
and through the beloved
lead us to more abundant life!

Bark is the surface
where gods appear to stir
the dreamer: a world wakes
under closed eyelids.

RED CAMELLIAS

Red camellia blossoms
the size of her hand
ride on wind
outside her window.

Sound of car tires
crunching gravel:
she closes blinds
steps into the foyer.

Behind her, a door
with a sign: *Cave canem.*
A room used for laundry
now houses her dogs

while she entertains a mysterious man
they have heard but never seen.
Her movement toward the door
stills them, makes them go

suddenly quiet
like guinea fowl used to do
on the farm
where she grew up

when any neighbor
intruder or marauder's approach
would make the yard's hush palpable
and warn the household.

She is sure the royal Pekingese
intimate companions of home
and heart who guard her
as if she were an empress

are signaling silently
to each other now

that *he* is here:
the one who calls

by day and night
and is received in privacy.
The tawny one declares
that he intrudes

disturbs their peace.
The dark one mutters
"Marauder! and she likes it!"
And so they whisper-growl

while he stays an hour or two
then leaves her full of love
and dreams from which
she offers them

when they resume their roles
as Most Important Ones
pats and strokes and tummy rubs
without the baby talk

eyes aglow, watching
red camellias blow.

HAIR COMBING

Just out of bed, when lovingly I say
that your hair looks tousled
and run my fingers through the locks
you take my comb from the dresser
and without wasted motion
bring your hair to order.
Standing so near my face
still flushed with excitement
from kisses and licks and caresses
suddenly your eyes open wide
and take me in again.
You begin to comb my hair
from the middle part
drawing tortoiseshell tines
down the hair's full length
to my shoulder
(and I begin to turn)
as you move
along the back
slowly, slowly
crown to tip
slowly
keeping love's rhythm
with me
under your hand
rising to your touch
coming near my right ear
and to the front again
deftly stranding every hair.
Only when each has been
laid lovingly beside its kin
when you have seen them all in place
and all have felt your concentrated gaze
do you unlock your eyes
and let a smile break out across your face.

GOLDEN ORB WEAVER

The long heat and drought have made me wonder
    if there will be any fall this year at all. I study
the orb weaver's web outside my window
    where she of the golden abdomen has found
a wandering wasp and bound it in her silk pantry to eat
    when she must, thereby showing how life
and death belong to the same appetite.

In my morning room where I lie in bed
    with my lover, there's lots of heat
but no drought—plenty of slaked thirst—
    then I'm off to spin the orb of my day, first
to get a mammogram. He says to tell the technician
    that he's already examined my breasts
and finds both perfectly sound … and lovely.

At the aptly named Webb Center for Women
    they're set to speed me through unwelcome
handling: attempts to flatten breasts and make them
    look like giant pancakes, each with a strawberry
on the side, to radiate them and see if cells
    are hiding aliens that might overpopulate
the space and rob me of my job, my life.

Technicians all call me by my first name each time
    they speak with bold voices and perky smiles
and winks and "Come on, girl, we're going to get
    you in and out of here in a hurry." Unlike
the orb weaver's death-dealing quest for food
    their job is to save me from death by reading
danger signs the human eye can't always see

though I think my love who cocoons me in his long arms
    strengthens my immune system enough to ward off
most threats to my well being. His unwavering attention
    is the best treatment I know for anything that ails me.
Then I am on my way to Ann's condo where she sleeps

her last big sleep and wakes now and then
to search for lost thoughts that no longer arouse her.

I put my hand on her shoulder tucked beneath
the sheet. "Ann," I say. "Do you want to wake up
for awhile?" She cannot move her head but cuts her eyes
toward me. "Sure," she says. *My beloved muse*
she calls me, with light emotion but sincere, as is each
fragment of a thought or image coming dryly
from her mouth. *A dry soul is best*, Heraclitus says

warning against the worldly pleasures that make it moist.
And yet, sweet-souled Ann! I am sorry to see
you so dry, so husk-like as I sit on your bed leaning
over you, and you look around as far as you can see
in your stillness and acknowledge me and stay awake
until I say you can sleep if you want to, and you do.
Welcome sleep.

My intent was to read you D. H. Lawrence's
Ship of Death poem and help you build one
of your own, laying out a scarf as ship and filling
it with an acorn, a stick of cinnamon, a flower
a piece of chocolate, an eye of God
and whatever you might add to see you
through the soul's dark night

but your thoughts are not in that direction
and so I leave the items there with your
beloved Ruth in case you wake enough and
want to make these preparations.
Ruth says you have already dreamed
of a houseboat, and so we are optimistic
that you have your vessel in harbor.

It takes time to cross town again in
rush-hour traffic, but never mind

I am entertained by radio news
        and find fresh irony in a report
of an execution scheduled for today
        that got postponed when the inmate
attempted suicide this morning.

Get this straight, if you can:
        his required death by lethal injection
was postponed because he tried to kill
        himself. His lawyers now are arguing
that he is incompetent to be put to death.
        So many deaths.
So many incompetent deaths.

Somewhere it is autumn
        and for travelers like Ann
the long journey toward oblivion
        is almost over, after which
I believe
        (as D. H. Lawrence does)
the soul wakes to a new dawning.

At home, I pause to peer at the gossamer
        web, grown vaster since I saw it last.
The wasp is gone, no doubt
        transmembered into silk.
That image leads me to petition my own fate:
        Like the golden orb weaver, let me spin
my life into a silken thread of desire

long enough and strong enough to lure me
        to my lover's lips again and again and again.
That is our only triumph over incompetence
        meanness, isolation, death:
to love well, with a trace of death in each embrace
        our only stay against heaven and hell
our only chance for more abundant life.

SNAPDRAGONS

Already, the summer morning is hot.
Snapdragons are lying back
with open jaws that seem to gasp
a small cough against the day's dry promise.
I stretch the water hose to send
a jetstream that will reach crape myrtles
whose tiny buds squeezed between
two fingers flower like
a woman's most intimate part.

The phone rings.
My hello is answered by your voice
as clear as if you were near enough to kiss
instead of two thousand miles abroad
emerging from a morning spent
touring a cathedral built
five hundred years ago.

And then I hear your *Cock a Doodle Do*
that I swear could fool a hen
or win audition for a movie soundtrack
like the cock I heard yesterday
in a film, circa 1965, crowing to herald
the Pope's return to Rome from battle
circa 1510 when he urged Michelangelo
to finish painting the Sistine Chapel ceiling.

I think of you and all the animal sounds
you make, so at ease in your animal skin
yet how you love your human life
as much as Michelangelo's Adam
holding out his hand to take
the quickening touch of God
and how you would wait for God to create
the one who would become for you

not helpmeet, but paramour, whose ear
would hear your cock's crow
ring out across a morning
centuries—no, millennia—later
proving that time and space spin out
of eternity to make moments like
the thrill I feel even when you
are an ocean away, traveling into my ears
on sound waves that touch
down deep in my rib-ringed heart.

My eyes start tears.
Words gush how much I miss you.
You miss me more than you love cathedrals
you say, more than anything:
a hundred times a day you see me
touch me in your mind.

My dangling hand that longs
to reach across the miles
instead
spurts water on snapdragon roots
delays their death while
your voice quickens my anticipation:
soon you will return
to take my hand and all of me
into the house
the cool darkness where we will
recreate the body of our love.

SYNTAX OF LOVE

Love talk begins inside you
under the influence of another language
circulates around my image

and arrives on your tongue
already formed as a poem:
I will remember, when I drink this tea, you.

Not tea I made
but made by you, for me
because I like to sip hot tea

with milk the way you make it
and bring it in a flask
and set it on my table before

you gaze into my eyes
and drop to your knees
to touch my feet with reverence

warmed by passion that rises like a flame
to lick my lips, eager to make
one fire hot enough to smelt our gold.

When I am lying down
you stand lingering
to look at me

wearing only the ring you gave me
and in my ears, golden circles
that tangle in my hair.

You say
When I see you in your all-beauty
I am amazed.

Your eyes
unjaded by fashion or flash
can still see the world's first morning

first man and woman walking together
naked in the rain and rolling
among the earth's first lilies

smeared with pollen
drenched with deepdown scent
that sharpens breathing

as you press close to me
with eyes like foxes
bright and brown

intensely focused
on my eyes,
making nostrils flare:

all this, face to face
and conscious, human that you are
so rich and complex and purely giving.

How can I not then give you my gold:
golden lamplight on my forehead
lips and breasts and thighs

unfolding the sacred sex flower
the golden goddess who comes
to make us tremble and cry out

the golden tone of my voice
when I call your name and say
you are wonderful, I adore you

and you, lying on my breasts, whisper
Your cry of joy soothens me,
makes soft corners in my heart.

That is how, like the first ones to love
 we re-create each other
even as we rejoice in our unmaking.

I will remember, when I drink this tea, you.

FOX EYES

We are talking casually about the weather:
how long it may take trees to shed their leaves
and stand barelimbed before us.

You say
Think of it! every tree that is not an evergreen
drops every leaf.

Each tree begins its own big life
a hundred times as big as the life of a human
inside a seed small as an acorn, then

unfolds trunk and branches and twigs
and all these leaves that fall.
Every spring, they come again.

And we ourselves cannot make a single leaf
though we are nurtured from the same soil.
It is amazing.

And I say
The only other thing I've heard you
call amazing is sex.

And you say
but for the power of sex
do you think the world would be like this?

You are referring, of course, to
the abundance of budding
you just described with wonder

and all the patterns in nature
not to the mechanically transmitted
reports of human nature gone awry that

leap and dart and fly at us over the airwaves
to land in our living rooms
every waking moment that we tune them in.

You say
It is sunshiny and a small wind
is circling the leaves

and the sun shines on the leaves
circulating not swift like a tornado
but small, and it is beautiful to look at.

Knowledge of the heart
grows out of you like
green seeds sprout in dark soil.

Nature unfolds exquisite leaves
of brown and gold and red to color your life
with warmth and wealth and passion

leaves that fall on me, enrich my life
and come back green
ready for that journey all over again.

Later you say
I want only your love
to live happily in this world.

Now we are talking about dying.
You formulate this question: *when I die*
and people are gathered around me

and you are one of them
where do you think
my eyes will be?

On my tits
I say
and you agree

and then you say
back where I come from, we used to joke
that even when the fox dies

his eyes will be always
on the chicken shed.
That is how I am about you.

YOUR LAUGHTER

You are among
the most fortunate of men
to have a body that moves

through the world
in a state
of relaxed alertness

ready at any moment
to make with others
a community of lovers

and when your laughter rings out
no one alive can resist
the temptation to kiss you

and taste whatever
makes you so happy
warm and wonderful.

It is belongingness
you say:
a feeling of belongingness.

NIGHTRIDING

sometimes in sleep, dreamless,
our bodies close
front to flank

we forget our human faces
night holds us still
until

a hand of its own accord
moves half an inch along
a hip

curved high
between navel and knee
we turn

my breasts are snug
beneath your scapulae
(some say vestiges of wings)

like bears
we rouse ourselves
by growl and sniff

our hands declare us
human then
and in

our glad meeting
we fall away
from time

grow light and lift
in flight that takes us close
as we can get

to congress with the gods

III.
LOST AND FOUND

CHANGING ROOM

Nature invites the human eye to see
a chrysalis as a changing room, a pod:
a place where death and dawn agree.

Winged Psyche stretches wide and free.
A serpent sheds old skin against the sod.
Nature invites the human eye to see

a fallen seed unfold a massive tree.
From oaken arms, a hooting owl, loud:
a place where death and dawn agree.

And when we plunge our hands into the sea
hidden pearls are pried from oysters, flawed.
Nature invites the human eye to see

a spider spin its inwards into three
skeins of silken net, strong and broad:
a place where death and dawn agree.

Turning inside out is destiny:
Metaphors make the body of God.
Nature invites the human eye to see
places where death and dawn agree.

TRANSCENDENTAL

White clouds drift slowly
across the blue domed sky
as I motor north by northeast around
Atlanta toward a building

where I am going to be crowned
by the steady hands of my dentist who
when it comes to mouth management
holds my absolute trust.

I window-watch clouds even as I drive
thinking how the absence of these sky vistas
brought me home again after ten years in New York City
where highrise buildings choke the view

to live once more South under what we call the heavens
implying more than one, though I am sure we don't
often think that through. Nonetheless, deep thought often
rules in favor of multiplicity.

I like to pause sometimes in my long look
into the deeps to recognize that **up** is a valid view
and one we don't want to lose in our quest
to compensate centuries of neglecting **down.**

Cloud-gathering Zeus directs my window drama
shaping dense clusters we call cumulus
with cirrus feathers that break away
leaving blue tremors in the atmosphere

as I nose my car toward a different kind of skyrise:
the medical center appears above a treeline on a hill.
Entering, I elevate to the fifth floor, check in and sit
in the dental chair facing a wide window

where, for a moment, I see the same sky Michelangelo saw
when he shaped both Adam and God, with
fingers reaching out to fingers, unfurling the world
on a canvas of blue and white, dropcloth of creation.

But now—perhaps because I am still and listening to jazz
on a special tape made by my dentist to entertain himself
while he works on teeth and gums, and to entertain his
patients, too, of course—the drama changes:

In the sky I see great beasts with gray bellies.
One elephant's trunk curls gracefully around another's
broad head while weightless they stomp their way
through the blues of a festive day in New Orleans.

My dental work gives me time at last to settle patiently (yes)
into the mood of Han-shan in China where Buddhist
monks were called cloud-wanderers. He asked, *Who can leap
the world's ties and sit with me among the white clouds?*

These cumulus clusters practice shapeshifting dances
while cirrus fingers reach here and there
like God and Adam or wandering monks
(or particles and waves) giving body to a world.

Now, in my body, the drama of bonding is hushed.
With hands still enough to steady the world, my dentist
holds the crown in place until, once upon a time
time out of mind, I am here and there

everywhere and nowhere.
And when one of the cloud-wanderers says
Show me your face before your parents were born
I reply, *Look here!*

much to the amazement of Dr. Mark
whose own quiet reverie must have included
elephants, from the way his trunklike arm and hand
draw back to see if my crown holds steady
and whether my outcry has anything to do with any ***thing***.

WOMAN WITH A BOWL OF GRAPES

Hair white and kempt, hand clamped on her fork
she pushes at one of five grapes in a small white ceramic
bowl beside her plate. After ten minutes I offer her a spoon

and make with it a small scooping motion.
She glances at me, blue-eyed, slowly shakes her head
and looks away again to try the grape

as though forking one could stop the willful passage
of time, break open the fading world and spill
its sweetness once more along her tongue.

BODY OF GOD

On a cold gray December day, just right for an adventure
in color, I set out with my friend Manta to see
the Dali exhibition at the High Museum of Art
in Atlanta. We aim to get there as close
to ten as we can. I have chosen this day for our outing
because it is free day for Fulton County residents
and next to spending money lavishly from time to time
Manta likes nothing better than a bargain
unless it's something free. *Frugality is how*
you get the funds for generosity is part of her
philosophy. She has lived a long and frugal life
full of generous gestures that prove her point.

First, we drive some distance to find Pearle Vision
where new spectacles are waiting that may help her
see more Dali details, even though at 93, her eyes
are keen, and she can read the phone book but doesn't
find much of interest there, she says. The optometrist
a woman with an Eastern European accent
is generous in her attention, and after Manta says that one
of her ears—Manta's ears, I mean—is higher than
the other, she patiently bends the frames an iota at a time until
they are perfectly balanced across Manta's nose
and we can leave, with my companion cheerfully counting
how much she saved by traveling all this way.

Now we are headed toward Dali, I know, but life is not
after all a straight line, and digressions interest me
as I think through how it is that life and art go along
with each other in this century we were not born
in but will surely die in, leaving only traces of what we
know and feel and make of our lives. Snug in my
Acura, rolling down the Interstate, Manta tells me
a dream about a lion in the front seat of her dream
car, facing backwards toward where she is sitting, and
we talk of dreams and agree that animals are
important visitors, even if we don't know what they mean
like the dove that flew out of a box she

opened in another dream. I say I have one to tell her
later, but now I have to exit, and Look! There's
the tent for the Cirque du Soleil. She says she bets it's cold
in there, and I say that it only appears to be a tent
and has heating the same as the buildings all around, though it
looks different with its low-slung turban shape. I tell her
how I like to see the circus, where performers explore limits
of what the human body can do, set up there among
skyscrapers, breaking up the stern business look of all
those rectangular prisms, and drawing the eye down
in a spiraling whirl of blue and yellow toward the ground.
She agrees it's an eyeful of contrast and looks pretty there.

In the museum parking lot I let her out next to the elevators
and park and catch the level 3 and stop at 4 to pick her up
and go on to 5 where we emerge and walk with our elevator
group across the courtyard. Mindful of the cold, Manta
is wearing a red wool jacket over a gray top above her black
trousers and looks artful herself, as do I, dressed in black
tunic and pants under a velour duster laid out like an abstract
painting in large red and black horizontal waves.
We take ourselves through the revolving door with others who
also have twinkles in their eyes, as if this movement
toward art has aroused in them an expectation that something
good, something worth our time, is about to happen.

Sure enough, we get in free after I show my ID to two Asian
ladies whose inspection we have to pass, along with copies
I have brought of Manta's driver's license, which has her old
address along with her social security card sent to the new
address in the right location to qualify for this free admission.
Now, a wheelchair for her to reduce fatigue that goes
with museum tours in old and young alike. I mentioned that
the check-in ladies have an Asian look, as I said the optometrist
had an Eastern European accent, to point up the new mix of Atlanta
culture, created in the past decade's flow of immigrants
directly into the middle class, sophisticating our color palette
and making multifarious the timbre and pitch of voices.

Today, the atmosphere is full of *Espagnol.* Manta says,
Have you noticed all the men? I look
around and apprehend a sea of masculinity. These are
phenomena I can't account for among stereotypes
that say American-born men spend winter Sundays
watching football games, and Latino immigrants
work all the time, mostly in construction and in yards.
It's got to be the Dali draw, the Eros factor:
lure of the illusionist, desire of the public to be tantalized
tickled, tittilated, teased, taken out of ourselves—all
reasons Manta and I are here instead of home sleeping
late on Sunday morning.

We move with a small crowd into the first room
full of photographs from Phillippe Halsman's book
showing Dali sporting with his moustache in a hundred
ways, shaping it like a bow or dollar mark, creating
an illusion that he is suspended in air by two threads of hair
on either side of his lip. The show is densely packed.
We choose to forego lingering among the photographs
that we can see in a book, and anyway, they are full
of buffoonery, which might be entertaining on another day
but what we want today is to see what makes the world
take this moustache-tugging, mirror-mugging, time-melting
show-off seriously.

The *New York Times* critic says that each piece of Dali's work
in the Atlanta exhibition is a "furious little world," and I agree
that here are worlds upon worlds and worlds within worlds to be
explored by two such cultural adventurers as we imagine ourselves
to be on this fine day in the city. In 1976 I traveled to a rural town
in South Carolina to board a Pullman car and see
a traveling bicentennial exhibition of mineral sculpture designed
by Dali and made under his direction, with precious stones
brought in from remote places and fashioned into exquisite
scenes and pieces arranged in little dioramas, each
with its own light. Dazzling. That was then and still is now
among the most astonishing art experiences of my life.

And though this High Museum show was curated
with an academic premise that *late Dali*, defined
as *Dali since 1940,* is not synonymous with *bad*
Dali (an opinion held generally in the art world
since he left the Surrealists in the l930s and declared
himself a classicist and became a celebrity
and clowned endlessly in performance art and got himself
on the covers of innumerable magazines
two dozen copies of which are framed and on display
here), we are less interested in the academic approach
or the Pop Dali presentation than in those furious little
worlds of the paintings that pull us to them.

We decide to tour without audiotapes because
they will distract us from seeing for ourselves
and anyway we can read the text on the wall next
to the paintings. By deft management of Manta's
wheelchair and a choreography of movements
in which I bend over her shoulder to whisper
questions and comments, and swing aside
to stand from time to time, we are able to get
close to the art work without annoying others.
Creeping deep into a crescent of viewers, we
are suddenly in front of the 10 X 14 inches of Dali
dynamite mentioned by the curator as the catalyst

for Dali's fame. So small! Manta recounts the story
she read about the artist at home alone looking
at a landscape he'd painted and wondering how to make it
fantastic when he noticed the Camembert cheese
on the table had begun to melt and thought of time and melting
and made the piece we see here, which his wife
Gala, when she came home, said would be unforgettable
to anyone who saw it and gave him the idea to call it
The Persistence of Memory. Manta wants to know what
that is in the middle of the picture, and I confess I do
not know though it has one closed eye with eyelashes and appears
to be dreaming. Perhaps it is Dali, I say, or the mind

of Dali looking raw and washed up from the sea. (Later I am
embarrassed to discover on looking at another Dali painting
in a book that the image does not refer to Dali's mind at all
unless to fantasy. The other title makes clear that the single
eye of this object is strictly male and located well south of the face.
I point to the cluster of ants on a timepiece and tell Manta
I read that he often puts ants into his paintings as a symbol
of death and also of female genitalia. Manta says she
has heard that frogs symbolize the female part and if the lady down
the hall where she lives knew that, she probably wouldn't
crowd ceramic frogs around her door.
Unless, of course, she's Daliesque, is my reply.

Before going on to *gravitas,* I'll mention that we drew
close to a sample of Dali's playing in his genius way
with Benday dots years before Roy Lichtenstein did. The
Sistine Madonna is a blowup of a newspaper photograph
of Pope John XXIII's ear, with the correspondingly large pattern
of halftone dots. Inside the ear, Dali painted
his version of Raphael's 1613 *Madonna and Child.* We don't ask
What was the point? but note that he tried out techniques
taken up later by Lichtenstein and Warhol, among others.
Experimenting, playing, joking, laughing: all part
of the mercurial mind and the intelligent hands behind what
we see here, shaped no doubt by celestial humor.

The curator also says that Dali wrote a 1960 essay called
The Divine Cheese in which he declares that Christ was made
of cheese. One starts to smile at this outrageous antic thought,
until one hears a little more about the source: Book 9 of
St. Augustine's *Confessions.* Augustine, God rest his soul, read
a passage quoting Psalms 67:22-3 where Christ is referred to
as that mountain flowing with milk, that fruitful mountain, which
in Latin was given as *monte incaseato*, literally the "mountain of
curds" for which the Latin Vulgate uses the word *coagulatus*
whose original meaning was "cheese," leading St. Augustine
as the story goes to read the passage as mountain of cheeses and thus
to describe Christ as a *mountain of cheese*, just as Dali did.

If anything can be everything, what then? There's some allure
in the correspondences here. Dali was born the same year as
my father, in 1904. Synchronicities carry the implication that
people and events that coincide in time can travel over long
distances in space to partake of each other. My father and
Dali were not totally unlike, each one fond, let us say
of altering his state of mind through drink or drugs
as often as the impulse struck. And they both were
unconventional, rebellious, and unpredictable. Come to think of it
both were painters! My father was very proud of his
skill as a housepainter and didn't flinch when he was asked
to climb and paint the water tower in the town, a task

I'm sure Dali would have loved and would have devised for it
some strange and wonderful show to thrill milltown folks
in Aragon, Georgia, circa 1927. Now look at that coincidence!
My birthplace was named for an Atlanta Hotel
which was named after a town in Spain where Dali lived.
Still, I am sure he was not my father, and for that, I am
no doubt grateful. Dali called several men including Freud *his* father
though I think he is closer to Jung in his expression
of the archetypal world; it is clear that he ingested many
influences and made them all—into Dali. I wonder
whether his symbolizing comes entirely from whim or sometimes
at least from a deeper look at the interface between

nature and art, though neither Manta nor I can think how
ants resemble the place that frogs do look somewhat like.
However, we both are wise like Socrates in that we know
a little about how much we do *not* know. And so, we go on
without excessive intellectual strain over these matters.
We are now in front of the 4 foot 9 X 3 foot 1
Madonna de Port Lligat from 1950, in which Dali distorts
his figures, not like Picasso into a cubist arrangement
but in his own way, retaining a figurative style while disturbing
our perception of people and religious icons
and even nature all at once. Here, Gala as the Madonna levitates
more or less inside an arched stone niche suspended

above the water in six pieces close enough together that one can see
their full shape around her, and her with fingers touching
in an attitude of prayer, face tilting to her right and eyelids
closed. Just above the voluminous skirt of her lap
and framed by a door that looks through Mary's chest to the sky
beyond, sits the Christchild, arms floating to the side
with a ball under his right hand and a book under his left, head
down, one leg folded under the other, outstretched, himself
with a door in his chest, where Manta locates a piece of bread
but we do not exclaim what might be expected to pop
out of the mouths of Southern ladies untutored in Catholicism—
things like, What on earth is he doing with a piece

of bread where his heart ought to be? No, we are way
too sophisticated for that kind of effrontery, and eventually
we conclude that it is the *bread which is my body* that we
one-time Protestants are familiar with as a wafer.
Above Mary's head is an ostrich egg, traditional symbol of the Virgin
because it was believed that the ostrich let her egg hatch
in the sunlight, without intervention, and so suggested
the immaculate conception, which, according to one student
taking a humanities class exam, is something Catholics do.
Around the Madonna and Child are other symbolic items: fish
bowl, folded cloth, shell, flower and—of all things—a rhinoceros
painted on the cabinet beneath the Virgin's foot. I have read

that Dali was fascinated with the logarithmic spiral he found
naturally occurring in the shape of a rhino's horn. I want to clap
my hands and do. Look, Manta! It's a rhinoceros!
She, who has not read the same article, thinks that perhaps
I have overreacted. But she'll change her mind later on
when she sees what I am excited about. Now we move
to *Christ of St. John of the Cross*, nearly seven feet tall.
It is a God's eye view from above looking down on a figure
suspended vertically against a cross (impossible perspective!)
crafted carefully to show the musculature of youth
in shoulders, arms, upper back and neck, from whom
the nails and crown of thorns have been removed and who

appears to be floating in tandem with the cross instead of fixed
to it, high in a dark sky above the bay of Port Lligat
in Catalonia. The head of the figure falls forward
so we can't see his face, but we imagine him to be
handsome, to embody a fullness of life that we hate to lose. His
head makes a circle inside the triangle of his arms and the cross.
I am thinking: How clean! How fine! How real! And how different
from the realism so often seen in this icon, where nails
and thorns pierce flesh, and blood runs, and vinegar gets
poured into open wounds, as in Mel Gibson's movie
where the Christ is grimy, sweaty, bloody and painful
to look at and incites hatred toward those who made him

suffer. Here, with the Dali Jesus, one doesn't flinch
or cry or grind one's teeth while looking on suffering
and death but instead, one stands contemplative in what James Joyce
called aesthetic arrest. And that is perhaps the most
propitious frame of mind for practicing forgiveness and all
the other Christlike virtues we are encouraged to imitate.
Many years ago in Washington, D.C., I stood before the monumental
Dali Crucifix looking up toward Christ on the cross
deeply moved and marveling at the classic painting skills.
Manta and I notice that Dali likes to create
perspectives that seem impossible to render on a flat surface.
I say I have heard him called a freakishly fine

draftsman, and Manta says so has she. Some of these
paintings have homes in Japan, Canada, Scotland
and are pilgrimage sites. I believe that this one, housed
in Scotland, was voted that country's most beloved
painting. Dali said he had a cosmic dream in 1950 in which
he saw what he would paint and that it would represent
the nucleus of the atom and then he came to think
that Christ was the unity of the universe.
This dream and this idea are at the heart of nuclear mysticism
a term that captures Dali's interest in quantum physics
and Catholicism, so richly expressed in this exhibition
but so little discussed elsewhere though

forward-thinking writers like Joseph Campbell
and Karen Armstrong are pointing out resemblances
for example in the original Person imagined by Hindu yogis
who splits himself in two to make a companion woman
and from the two of them all of creation comes—the resemblance
of that myth to the physics of particle and wave that
occupies some of the best scientific minds today. Do particles cluster
to form us as individuals? we ask, and conclude, Then it must be
through waves that we are united with the All. That view reflects Eros
and spirituality, as well as science, and our minds are about to be
blown by the 7 1/2 by 4 2/3 foot *Assumpta Corpuscularia Lapislazulina*
an elongated rendering of Mary's bodily assumption, showing

a realistic, bust-like figuration of a haloed Gala-as-Mary, above arms
folded and fingers laced, above a geometrical space
in the area of the heart, above a small painting of Dali's
St. John of the Cross Jesus in the area of the womb
above a skirted altar containing three iconic crosses, above feet
pointing to or rising from a sphere that looks like a globe
but is a hydrogen atom that has exploded, releasing these forms
of Mary whose body is crystalline, gelatinous, whose robe billows
and breaks on either side into … rhinoceros horns.
See? I say knowingly to Manta who, true to character
is delighted to learn what strange things occupy the mind of genius.
The rhino horn motif is interesting but takes a back seat

to Manta's comments given when I wheel her toward the painting:
*Look how she is coming apart and disappearing
piece by piece.* To which I say that I guess that's how he
envisioned death. She goes on, *And when we come
apart, we flow into some other form and make something new!
You see, she does not completely disappear.* So Manta says better
than I can what those of us who meander among mythological
fragments wonder about and speculate on and tend to leave
in the realm of mystery. The greatest painting in history, in the opinion
of one blogger on the Internet, is Dali's *Santiago el Grande,*
an overwhelming 13 and a half by 10 foot work where
onlookers hovering near it seem small by comparison.

Again we see, rising up out of the waters of Catalonia, an explosive
sequence of images dominated by the splendid horse on which
St. James, patron saint of Spain where he is called Santiago
sits barebodied with his left arm raised to brandish not a sword
but a crucifix as large as he is, all being shot toward the heavens
from a nuclear cloud visible underneath the horse.
Our point of view is compelled to follow all this energy up
around them through a vaulted frame ornamented with scallop
shells, 12 of them as in the 12 disciples surrounding the figures of St. James
and Christ. Angels are patterned like wispy clouds
in the magnificent sky, floating diagonally from the neck of the horse
heavenward. We notice, too, the exposed sole of one foot

belonging to St. James, the dirt on it suggesting a lifetime of walking
in the world. In the bottom right corner, counterbalanced
on the left by a rocky land mass, stands Gala, robed and revered.
Dali said that through Gala he could see and render nobility
so it is a noble scene on a grand scale with the most unusual
perspective we've looked at, this time from underneath
the heavy, lovely Lippizanner's body where nuclear smoke curls
like rhinoceros horns to meet clouds that carry the color we
call heavenly blue. Oh! Is it possible that Salvador Dali, showman
extraordinaire, who reinvented himself after 1950 while I was
growing up and who came to exemplify celebrity status and pop
art, has here, in this exhibition, healed the divorce between

physics and metaphysics in the modern age? Does this narrative
fit the mold of the fairy tale in which the trickster/fool
holds the key to the kingdom and is the only wise one in it?
We decide we can't answer those questions until we've had
a cup of coffee, and so we go out and around and down until we find
a corner café where we can get not only coffee but a sweet as well.
I settle Manta at a table and go to the service counter and order
coffee and a large brownie for her and a chocolate scone for me.
When the server asks if I am a member, I frown, recalling
that I have not renewed my membership, and tell her
"not now" and she pauses a moment before she says I can be
a member for today and get my coffee free. You will know

by now how Manta enjoyed hearing that, and how she relished
besides the brownie, the dream I had been waiting to tell
her in which she and I were in the back seat of a car being driven
by my son who stopped beside the road where there was a load
of firewood because he knew that she and I as well as he would like
to collect it and where, underneath the pile we found two panels
of wood on which were carved the two sides of a large bird that we
thought was surely a phoenix because the wood was lightly
charred. The dream leads us to speak of rebirth in individuals and
in cultures, for of course we are sitting in a city that once
was consumed in a great conflagration. What we have now that we
didn't have when we came into the museum is a sense

of possibilities: invention, reinvention, death, rebirth from the ashes of all
that has come and gone. Endless possibilities in the endless
flow of coffee, chocolate, and conversation. We came at ten and now
it is two when we relinquish her wheelchair and walk together
back to the elevator. At the fourth floor I escort Manta out
to wait for me to drive around, then hurry back into the elevator
and declare to the others that I am not abandoning her. One woman
replies, "No, we wouldn't let you do that. She reminds me of my
mother, who is 93." Synchronicities abound when the psychic
climate is weathery, as it is on this day in December in Atlanta
when we travel back on Highway 75 North past the circus tent
that we now know follows Dali's beloved spiral shape and makes

a sacred space where, in this show called *Ovo* (Portuguese
for "egg") human performers represent insects, who do the most
remarkable things with their heads, torsos and appendages
not unlike what Dali does in his paintings. Manta removes her
spectacles and rests her eyes while we drive, musing on the near
century of her life, and I think of time melting and turning
into Manta's dream lions and doves, of ants and frogs, a phallus lying
like a used handkerchief on the ground, of Mary and Jesus and
Santiago and the Pope's Ear, of sexy and noble wife Gala, of the phoenix
bird we found. I think also of the various ways in which we all
are crucified in the tension of opposing forces in our lives and how
we can rejoice that we are made of particles and more
particles, waves, and possibilities.

MORNING GLORY

Forty years ago I buried my father
in the ground and in my heart.
Today he rose in my garden:

a morning glory vine that climbed a broken limb
leaning vertical against the wood fence
dangles a lavendar-fluted flower

like those we used to see unfolding
in the dawn dew on the massy vines twining
barbed wire fence and trailing tendrils

that he would touch and say
Look!
and I would spy beneath the leaves

a curl of color, crimson bleeding blue.
Our eyes would meet
and I would think his thought

(as I am this moment, now):
There is beauty in the world. Go out
of the house every day and find it.

No imperative but wonder filled his voice.
And I am still in love with the world
that still bleeds thrilling color to my eyes

shaped out of darkness
containing dawn and dusk
all places betwixt and between.

THE FEATHER

Fine featured and dark-cloud gray
lying on grass, molted
from a sky-surfing turtledove:

now a single instrument
humans collect
to make a brush or fan
or fun-weapon
(sometimes
for tickling
never
for hurting).

Raking you
so soft!
across my palm

I know you are
immeasurably light

to all except
the Egyptian dead
whose heart must be judged
lighter even than you before they
can enter the Fields of Peace.

Oh, weightless treasure
feather my heart!

LUNA MOTHS

I stand at my front door waving goodbye to you.
It is still morning, the light above the door
still on, and as you drive away

my one foot follows the other down three steps
as if I might catch you
until I catch myself and turn and see

on the door frame
two Luna moths side by side in a green glide
wing tips touching when they stop to rest

and to arrest my eye
and say
in their lovely soundless way

Hasten slowly through your life. There
may be more, but lose no part
of this miraculous luna green morning.

SWEETGUM TREE

When you place your hand
on a rough-barked tree in your front yard
like the sweetgum tree in mine, to stand
with it awhile, leaning, perhaps with some
longing toward an absent lover, can you
feel the tree touching you
in such a way that you know
its resistance will hold you
that you won't fall forward
or back or down, but can wait
without striving, held steady
by this figure whose fiber
seems so unlike your own
and yet so familiar
flourishing there, so close to home?

SOURCES FOR QUOTATIONS IN PREFACE

Joseph Dietzgen, *The Positive Outcome of Philosophy*, a 19th century text restored and presented by Andesite Press, 2015.

D. H. Lawrence, *The Body of God*, a sequence of poems selected and arranged by Michael Adam, with woodcuts by Barbara Whitehead. Dulverton (Somerset): Ark Press, 1970, p. 17.

Rudolph Otto, *The Idea of the Holy*. New York: Oxford University Press, 1958, pp. 5-8.

W. B. Yeats, *Stories of Red Hanrahan, The Secret Rose, Rosa Alchemica.* New York: MacMillan, 1914, p. 225.

Federico Garcia Lorca, "Arrow," *The Selected Poems of Federico Garcia Lorca*. New York: New Directions Publishing Corporation, 2005, p. 25.

David L. Miller, *Three Faces of God: Traces of the Trinity in Literature and Life*. New Orleans: Spring Journal, Inc., in collaboration with Pacifica Graduate Institute, Carpinteria, CA, 2005, pp. 156-7.

C. G. Jung, *Letters*, Vol. II, ed. Gerhard Adler. New Jersey: Princeton University Press, 1976, p. 436.

T. S. Eliot, *The Four Quartets.* New York: Houghton Mifflin Harcourt Publishing Company, 1971, "East Coker," Part V.

David Abram, *The Spell of the Sensuous*. New York: Random House Vintage Books, 1997, pp. 270-1.

Susan Rowland, C. G. *Jung in the Humanities: Taking the Soul's Path*. New Orleans: Spring Journal Books, 2010, p. 85, with reference to Ann Baring and Jules Cashford, *The Myth of the Goddess: Evolution of an Image*. London and New York: Penguin Arkana, 1993.

John O'Donohue, *Anam Cara*. New York: Harper Perennial, 2004, p. xvi.

Barbara Knott has a Ph.D from New York University's drama therapy program. While in New York, she studied acting with William Hickey, famous for his classes at the Herbert Berghof Studio in Greenwich Village and for his character roles in Hollywood films like *National Lampoon's Christmas Vacation* and *Prizzi's Honor*. She also did extensive work in theater and in Montessori education for pre-schoolers. On her return to Atlanta, she became co-director with her husband Charles of the Center for Archetypal Studies and served terms as program chair and then president of the C. G. Jung Society while practicing therapy for five years before entering a fulltime teaching career in English and humanities and settling into writing consistently in the happy company of Rosemary Daniell's Atlanta Zona Rosa writing group. Since retiring from teaching, she has given full attention to writing and collaborative arts performances and to editing and publishing *The Grapevine Art and Soul Salon*, online literary/art journal at www.grapevineartandsoulsalon.com and www.barbaraknott.net.

She says of her work: "I am interested in the world and its diversity of creatures and in what makes us human and in whatever lies in the depths of human experience, where oppositions lay down their arms, where the erotic meets the sacred, and where serious sits down with humor to sort it all out." And this: "My goal as a writer of fiction and poetry is to get the reader to feel part of an ongoing conversation I am having with myself about themes and images that appeal to my imagination, and to become as excited about them as I am."

In 2009 Barbara's poem "Boxwood" was selected by Judge Nikki Giovanni as first-prize winner of the *New Millennium Writings Awards 28* competition in poetry. Francois Camoin chose her short story "Song of the Goatman" as third-prize winner in the Writers at Work fiction competition in 2010. Barbara's first collection of poems, *Soul Mining*, a chapbook, was published in 2011 by Finishing Line Press.

In 2013 a poem "Apples in the Cellar of Dread and Desire" became a finalist in the short memoir competition held by Fish Publishing in Ireland. Her short story "The Legend of Abigail Jones" received first prize in the wild card category of Atlanta Writers Club's Spring 2014 competitions. Another chapbook, *MANTA Poems*, came out in March 2015, also published by Finishing Line Press. Barbara was selected with a group of poets to represent FLP as readers at the Abroad Writers' Conference in Dublin, December 2015.

CPSIA information can be obtained
at www.ICGtesting.com
Printed in the USA
LVHW04s0434060718
582857LV00004B/6/P